CONTENTS

I

12/8/92

To Mike,
Good seeing you.
Best wishes,

Any One Man

by

Roy Bentley

Midwest Writers Series
BOTTOM DOG PRESS
Huron, Ohio

ISBN 0-933087-23-3 (pap) / 0-933087-24-1 (cloth)

Acknowledgments

Poems in this collection have appeared previously in these magazines:
ARTFUL DODGE: "A Place to Come Back to," "The Picture My Father
Promised"; CINCINNATI POETRY REVIEW: "Lighted Jesus"; CONFLU-
ENCE: "The Love of the Long Married"; THE DEVIL'S MILLHOPPER:
"The Perfect Western"; IMAGES: "The Look on the Face of Man on the
Tractor," "1954," "Rowing in Eden," "Marciano," "On a September Morning
above a Pasture near Dayton, Ohio, Orville Wright Accomplishes His First
Figure Eight," "Trick of the Light"; INDIANA REVIEW: "View from the
Great Southern Hotel"; THE JOURNAL: "Giants," "The Baseball Wars,"
"The Gift of Fury," "Field of Stone," "Everyone Says So Who Claims to
Know the Story", "Notwithstanding a Love of the Truth Instilled in Her by
Her Father"; MID-AMERICAN REVIEW: "Dizzy Gillespie at the Blue
Note," "The Country of the Dead," "On Horseback D.V. Bentley Carries
Home News and Something More," "On Board the *Scirocco*, Errol Flynn
Asks John Barrymore Why Luck Follows One Man and Not Another," "The
Orchard the Dry Year"; NEW VIRGINIA REVIEW: "Bird and Miles"; PIG
IRON: "The Heart Has Its Reasons"; PIKEVILLE REVIEW: "Haying in
High Desert"; THE PLOUGH: NORTH COAST REVIEW: "The Edge of
Heaven"; THE REGULATOR: "Roman Polanski's *Chinatown*"; and RIVER-
WIND: "No Finish," "Letcher County, Kentucky" (first titled "The Effect on
Paradise of Our Collective Unhappiness").

A portion of this book appeared as the chapbook THE EDGE OF
HEAVEN published by Bottom Dog Press in Huron, Ohio in the
collection THREE BY THREE.
Grateful acknowledgment is made to the Ohio Arts Council for two
Individual Artist Fellowships awarded during the writing.
Special thanks to those who read the poems in draft stage: Bob Fox,
Daniel Bourne, Kate Hancock, Nate Leslie, Howard McCord, Claire
McCoy, Deni Naffziger, Bob Pond, Gloria Regalbuto, Larry Smith,
Dave Smith, Linda Gibbons Whetstone and others.

A very heartfelt thanks to Bob Demott for the push and shove and
affirmation offered during the course of the writing of this book.
And for his friendship.

Funded Through
Ohio Arts Council

III

For Matthew, Scott and Caitlin

Who, secretly, doesn't lust after every experience? It's late.

— Raymond Carver

I

Life isn't like in the movies.
Life...is much harder.

—Cinema Paradiso

The First Burning of Dreamland

Suddenly I am at the seashore
and no recollection of the train stopping...
                              —Henry Miller

The pain you know could be an elephant
named Topsy. Topsy's a man-killer.
Some guy's fed the damn thing a cigarette,
lit, but you've got to do something:
Sigmund Freud has had his picture taken
at the entrance to Dreamland.

Always the showman, you elect to execute.
You tell the New York papers it's death
by hanging. A partner commissions a scaffold.
The ASPCA says you can't hang an elephant.
All right, you say and hook him up.

A paying Coney Island public watches
the carny in the new suit loop two boots
of bare wire to yielded legs. Kinetascopes
roll. Tom Edison's kindest works—
incandescence and the motion picture camera—
labor to record the smoking six tons

going over, shitting and slumping.
It takes 10 seconds and feels, on review,
like the body of the thing was more fragile
than first appeared. Then, 2 A.M.,
hours before the season opens, Dreamland burns:

BEER-FOR-A-NICKEL signs, the hundred banners
announcing unencounterable worlds, ignite.
It begins in Hell Gate's long chutes of lathe.
Cheap fun has always burned, but tonight
braids of flame take DON'T BE A GLOOMSTER,

11

the pine braces of the Pavilion of Fun
threatened. Across Surf Avenue, Luna Park
holds its incandescent breath, a second
sister Eden itself vulnerable in starlight.

O Mr. Reynolds, Dreamland's one million bulbs,
its white tower, the Infant Incubator,
the Canals of Venice, the Train of the Future—
all lost to an overturned bucket of tar.
They'll say, for a century weary of the works
of its hands, that in a single day in 1911

200,000 postcards of the gartered fat woman
went out to Iowa, to Cleveland, Ohio
and wherever the Navies of the World
and the cascade of the lights of spectacle
lit a second night of imagination. In 1911
we are in love with the catch in the stomach.

We're watching, contemplating Dreamland.
We're glimpsing a clown's mouth in the coals,
phantom heads, Topsy's. It's down in minutes.
What's left is a waltz they'll never play,
a miraculously half-burned tent, acres of ash,
a last hanging ruin of a sign. The sign

might as well be the book of deepest night, any
we're suckered in by THE CONGRESS OF LIVING WONDERS.

The Country of the Dead

The vast country of the dead had its beginning
everywhere...
—Czeslaw Milosz

We sit in the panelled basement
Of his house in Ohio and listen
To a doctor in Sao Paulo sputter,
In perfect English, about ionic skip,
Waves of voice at the speed of light
Bounced, with little loss, day-to-night-

To-day. The room is radios and coaxial cable
At arm's length. A dark Zenith
He listened to the year I was born
Collects dust forlornly on a parts shelf.
Honolulu, he says, is nothing;
Biweekly, talks weather, rain or dry,

With Melbourne, Australia.
When I was a boy, seventeen,
Led Zeppelin albums spun between these walls.
Other atmospheres of marijuana smoke
Circled up and out through opened window wells.
Everything familiar

Was made over years ago, remodeled
And sealed to soundproof,
Antenna tower outside, above—
Where I scratched names, a heart, *Love Forever*—
Superseded, sold for scrap.
The handful of women who undressed

And let go mysteries below my parents' bed
Would never admit to so much of us
So scrupulously lost, one memory
Like another like something else or nothing
Very much must have happened here.

13

I want to ask the doctor in Brazil
What my father would think foolish:
Whether random connecting like this,
Continent to continent,
Ever goes beyond words and megahertz—
Talking air, my mother calls it.
I think of silence as message, whistling engine:

The bounty and emptiness,
Measured, looping adventure of electricity,
Bound in that lightning-becomes-voice instant
Of science and sense, all of it burning.
If there were call letters, a frequency
For the condition of hearts,

Signal would diminish in transit, an answer
Begin, *Say again.* The doctor
Speaks of the necessary death
Of rain forest to the north, of exports
And topless beaches. Says the trick
Is to look and not look.

Haying in High Desert

It's not so much the cold, impossible
  pull of spingwater
    drives you all day in the hayfields

as simple respect for a neighbor
  who, last year, ended a sullen month of this
    by stripping off and swimming

the Deschutes River at its swiftest point.
  Even his black Lab pup, shadowing
    at a distance, likewise knows enough

to earn the inevitable, longed-for dousing.
  All morning a twenty year old,
    fatherless, full of Ohio optimism,

hard promise, has set the pace
  at a dead run. Boys and grown
    and having much to settle, we work

as if the fight were for the shared good graces
  of our fellows and squared something.
    This one with the most to prove

calls from a wagonback. Offers a hand
  and I am up—
    twenty-three and at rest momentarily

above the bale-by-bale pure closing
  of labor, bright cobalt wing
    and hollow of sky

coming unevenly through a tease of cirrus
  then barn flooring, the latticework
    of rafters. This bronze Midwesterner

15

with the borderless confidence of youth—
   Jesus, and that typically American
     bullshit-glorious look

of no-matter-what-byGod—
   says nothing of his longing for the girl
     with hair the color of droughted fir

(Sandy or Sally or something) who'll
   cheat on him the instant he's out of Oregon.
     Sure, he'll see her tonight. Sure,

she'll make the whole bored, tired lot of us
   swallow when she closes the door
     to his room and laurel wreaths descend

beautifully disguised as kisses,
   the sudden perfection of cool sheets.
     It's good to wrestle haybales, soft

palms bleeding in the heat. Something
   toughens, the heart
     faces all the essentials as one flood

over which it has damned little influence.
   Still, tonight I'll lie awake
     and listen to pine and poplar

rough-hand the house. I'll have bathed
   in the Deschutes; and sure, hell,
     all the way to sleep I'll hear those two

cackle and coo and go silent, what
   passes for love splendid and upborne,
     sufficiently impure, small drama

played to sweet completion in the dry months.

The Look on the Face of the Man on the Tractor

At roadside a man has his hand in a woman.
Black, disordered skirtfolds pillow at hips.
Gentle petitioner, the woman kisses
Upward, mouthing the fire-eats-paper memory

Of assent and loss and no sound,
Wide, unflinching fields of surprise
At how completely and at midday
He has husked her.

Among uncut, uninclined grasses
A farmer steers to rutted road, light
Threading knowingly down
To those loosed from covering,

Unburdening below the hollows.
The farmer, atop this day's resonant machine,
Looks and again into that which binds him
To the thing itself: corrupting and corruptible,

Too public geometries of belly and hand,
Blood's deciduous thrilling.
If he is moved, reminded,
Wending himself mentally into like embrace,

It does not show. The old engine
Thrums bleached air and what is skin.
Little flamelets, lust and summer
Rage, rage and swell impossibly with the dust.

The Long Night Is Always about Love

There's a suffocating Perfect Joy to the air,
though we've left a wedding party
to stand outside in arc light and Pacific breezes.
You're telling me, confessing in starts and stops,
to having slept with a guy looks like Phil Donahue.
The panel truck I hit with my fist
then my whole body reads ISLAND CATERING.

The work of my body is, tonight, shudderingly
more real than the big wars of the century
and turns to shadowed waves of dents, the truck
more solid than I'm inclined to confess.
That afternoon we had bougainvillea, hibiscus,
star jasmine to walk beneath, through.
The Nikon cameras of the Japanese tourists

clicked like keys in new locks. Cliff divers
spoke to crowds from clefts in the rockface
like patron saints. (The saints were from Ohio.)
Now you say, *You were gone, You're married*
and throw back your head, your raised voice
become a singing, dark and patterned.
I want to slip easily from all this dread

of loss reduced to a chorus of surf.
I want to take the stainless steel scalpel
I catch you with on the cabana's concrete lanai
and show you how to rest the blade to do it right.
But the long night is always about love,
and instead I throw it, a low arcing toss,
into a bay named for turtles. The knife's

turning blazes in moonlight, the happy purposelessness
of blossoms everywhere—tamely journeying hedges
of hibiscus deadening the out-tide's quiet
spearing of the coast, low trees of starred
plumeria blooms that in the morning we trample,
without reflection or remorse, months before storms
islanders say God gave them to keep them guessing.

Like a hand on your hand, let all this
be a sign of something, I tell myself.
You could have dropped from the sky
like any of thousands of ripped blossoms
long before you saw the truth about suffering,
that its only shape comes from bonds
stronger than love. And flowering in the flesh.

On Board the *Scirocco*, Errol Flynn Asks John Barrymore Why Luck Follows One Man and Not Another

> *I enter a whorehouse with the same interest*
> *as I do the British Museum or the Metropolitan—*
> *in the same spirit of curiosity.*
> —Errol Flynn

Drunk, as usual, Flynn remembers the fighting
in Spain, death all around
and the terrible fear, the nightmare motion
of bodies stripped of breath and limb
in long instants. Barrymore
staggers aft in search of ice.
In his absence Flynn recalls

Dr. Gerrit H. Koets
leaning over the railing of a freighter
outbound from New Guinea. Dr. Koets
has just spoken of the boon sunlight is.
Naked by the rail, Koets
pounds his great chest and expounds
on the inherent animalism of women.

At the rail, daily,
Koets and Flynn become friends.
The two stop in the Philippines
and rent a hut. Koets
has an idea to fix cockfights
by putting little grooves into the beak
then adding a dab of snake venom
prior to the festivities: one bird
picks the comb of the other
and the poison is passed.

The idea tested, they lease the finest estate
overlooking Manilla Bay, buy clothes.
One night the magic works too well

and quickly, the opposition's cock
dying before the first tentative blow.
Flynn smiles at the memory of Koets
running, stick legged,
the *Empress of Asia* pulling away,
angry Filipinos
dockside, waving bolos.

From the blown spray, Barrymore reappears,
high-toned, quoting Rimbaud.
Tired of poles and zones, sometimes the martyred sea,
Rolling me gently on her sobbing breast
Lifted her shadow flowers with yellow cups toward me
And I stayed there like a woman on her knees.
Barrymore, trapped himself
in this perfect net of vanity and loss
and winning back less each trip out,
settles mid-deck, raises a double Scotch
in salute to whatever gods.

The casinos on the Street of Happiness
in Macao in 1932
were where the question of luck became clear.
Here, with Koets, Flynn
won at fantan, lost big,
was robbed of a stash of diamonds.
Broke, the pair joined the Hong Kong Volunteers
and fought advancing Japanese.
In four days, the two deserted,

travelled on forged papers, reached
Marseilles and the bordello district
where twice daily a donkey
mounted an accommodating French girl.
"Imagine," Flynn says, absently.

Stairways of water and sunlight open.
The huge foresail of the *Scirocco* blooms.

Luck and a Witness

How do we come to be men
and passing 10 milligram blue
generic Valium washed down
with beer or Diet Pepsi
on a backporch in Athens, Ohio?

In the yard below the porch
a seven-year-old and friends
palm pop flies, rough peach crates
broken into bases. Smoke
from the worst Mexican marijuana
any of us has inhaled this deeply
since high school or college
blossoms in the mouth
of whomever braves the question,
Are we trying to kill ourselves?

I'm speaking again of Rhonda Holland
getting naked in my basement
at the reading of a poem. Blond
and stunningly beautiful, she said
she was thanking me. Not

for having every Pink Floyd album
including the imports
but because I'd written down
how our lives were.

Call it luck. We laugh now
and down beers one of us says
(Greg Anderson is my witness)
is the choice of angels like Rhonda.
From a wicker chair I have a window

on China, a *Time* photo essay.
In the eyes of a monk in Yunnan
there's a look of unguarded acceptance.
He's standing by a pool table.

One of the novices, tattooed,
one of his tattoos a name,
has cut the Three Ball, no rails,
and sent 6000 years of culture
rolling forward with authority
into the 1/60th of a second
the Nikon sees—that Forever
and Once of red and numeral
says there's more to the shot
than stroke or position
or even knowing the table.
And so much green. Besides,

in the photograph the Three
won't ever, ever drop. Just be
on its way and perfectly
like a story that saves you, laughter
hanging in the Spring air,
hanging, trailing off
like a hit Wiffle ball.

No Finish

For Doug Barnett the winter and spring I learn to drive,
getting rid of my virginity is project and goal.
The day after he makes love to Janet Barnard, preacher's
daughter, on the front seat of his Plymouth Fury,
he says she has a powerful beginning and middle but no finish.
Driving the hilly Ohio two-lane between New Lexington
and Newark, slapping the big steering wheel, singing
Buddy Holly: *That Janet,* he says, *she wants your cherry.*
Ahead, a truck, oncoming, sullen, signals with high-beams.
A little drunk Doug jumps suddenly into the back.
The Plymouth coasts, holds the long straight, pilotless.
In self-defense I slide over, accelerate. Panicked,
I explain how we're only as far as decapitation fatalities
in Driver's Ed. Slouching, beer in hand,
he is Midwest collected, the Johnny Carson of dreams
trapped undiminished in dullness, every embellished story
similar roadway. Finally, as he has all spring,
he cries for his brother Billy whose thirty and three-quarter
years ended the previous summer on a rented floor
in College Park, Maryland. The night he rushed in, too late,
it stunned him, he says, how much blood and bone we are,
how *just like that* (and he snaps his fingers) we go.
I tell him I don't drive standards, that New Lex
is five miles, downshifting inevitable.
He crosses the seatback, settles in. Passing a bar and grill,
he remembers my innocence, at length describes a waitress
who, on her break, took him into the lot behind the Esso sign,
raised her skirt. *There. On that pile of tires.*
In twenty years he will have left here.
Oldest daughter battling cancer, lymphoma, he will drive her
to chemotherapy, may well recall Janet Barnard, the Plymouth,
whatever act it takes to propagate wonder.
For an hour, uninterrupted, the FM station will play Presley.
The east Virginia sky will be a tumbled blue, one
steady, infinite rotation, a sign calling us in.

First   Sex

The way Matt Dillon and Kitty were
on *Gunsmoke*——barely touching
but giving up something off-screen
in one of those Dodge House rooms
full of light and lace, clean—
that's how I pictured it. But she
was Columbian, menstrual, barely
spoke English beyond *Bethlehem*
for *Bentley*. Matt would have
never been in that silver Airstream,
days of dishes in a stopped-up sink.
He'd have touched his Stetson, said
Ma'am and rose, faintly smelling
of leather, horses, tin marshall's
star catching the light caught her—
hair, breasts, shoulders, dark
child-nursed circles of nipple.
I woke with a burning a week later.
Matt would have had Chester limp
on over to the Long Branch, fetch
a fifth and some kill-or-cure elixir,
then shot her, gentlemanly-like,
made it look as if she drew down on him
first. (He'd have had to: Honor,
that other bitch of a hired gun,
would have called him out.) It's
nearly twenty years, a million units
of penicillin later, but that's what I'm
doing in the street. We'll settle up
with Colts, Rosita, one of us riding off
better for living by a code binding
and more just than micro-organisms.
I'll give you that split second, sun
in your eyes, the dust of horses
settling on us dull as blood.

The Perfect Western

In a western once, Burt Lancaster
asked a kidnapped Mexican woman
why she was worth one hundred thousand dollars.
When she told him to go to hell,
he said simply, *Yes, ma'am. I'm on my way.*
Who wouldn't walk easily: Woody Strode,
arrows at the ready, everywhere at once,
Burt Lancaster at flank,
Lee Marvin cradling a .50 caliber?
It's as if we've always known the fragility
and flown in its face, stayed behind
at the bottleneck, no way out—
*Dynamite, not faith, will move that mountain
into this pass*—to give the woman an hour,
a chance. And when Jack Palance/Raza
has shot you in each shoulder,
is it not all you can do to keep from smiling?
Of course lives are B movies, finding
easy Good and swift horses.
Of course the last trick will involve
sage smoke, riding side-mount.
Of course through the narrow rock
come those you've yet to wound: Conchita,
the Whore; Frederico, whose aim has shown you
watching and waiting are never enough;
Raza, the leader of the war that goes badly.
It is Frederico you spot, wound
in his rein hand then the heart.
Conchita, when she slows, drops
like your dream of her, though the third horse
has its eyes blanketed and is through.
You climb. Lee Marvin has left it in your hands,
tossed you the water, his Winchester,
insinuating confidence, earned mission,

dispensations preferable to long life.
Of course you are dying.
It has come to this. You've
less than a minute. Both shoulders
river blood. Rock everywhere,
you breath for us all, take aim.

Bird and Miles

They have a way of talking, between bites
of fried chicken, Bird and this fine light-
skinned woman alternately eating a wing
and leaning to kiss Bird's naked thigh,
so that the taxi down to 52nd Street
fills with smacking. Bird, already high
on heroin, fans one famous hand
around the neck of a fifth, inhales
his favorite food from the loose fist
of the other. Asks Miles Davis, who's
19 at the most, does all this make him
just the least bit *uncomfortable.*
The woman, in light summer clothes,
a dress, heels, kneels down in daylight
until everything hums in the half heat
of the backseat. *Turn your head, Miles,*
Bird says, and Miles does. Hangs it
out the down window. Miles is wearing
the wide-lapeled suit Bird bummed last week
after pawning his own and a suitcase.
(The suit, too small, hadn't fit in the sleeves
or pants legs, and Bird had gone to the gig
at the Three Deuces looking ridiculous. Bird
played that night like he had on a tux.)
The woman fans a fly or bead of sweat
from her face. No one in the taxi
but she and Bird are moving, no one from
that other world outside where rain threatens.
Just this puffy-eyed, running-to-fat,
balding black man White America has heard of
or will. This woman practicing an art
thrills all those other interiors like a breeze
sudden through a room, even in the backseat
of a taxi traveling deeper into the heart

of the delta of 1945, New York City traffic.
Finally there, everyone moves--Miles,
Bird, the woman.   The driver who,
resetting the meter, watches Bird
the way you would anyone whose movements
call to mind a flame, purling, blue,
jumping in the astonished air above a stove
someone's lit and turned from.

Bird of Paradise

His face, all midnight and rough wonder
scuffling through the riffs, breaks
into a smile as if he's made a connection.
He sits for a while in the unholy smoke
haloing Lester Young. Lester's finished playing
and leads him from the bandstand. Bird's

asking how long the break is, sliding
his big end-of-the-road body
onto a stool. The eyes, two heavy pennies
in the pocket of God, look out
at the raw light of the Paradise Club sign
spilling across the world's body of tabletops.

The tabletops give back Bird's movements,
Lester's, in reverse, the way tired asses
appear in the hard harness of a life
after life. All right, he says.
They start back to their instruments, soul-
tired but looking out over a water of faces.

Someone says this bunch is the new dead
on which no tenderness has yet
been lavished. They lay down a stream of notes
that pushes past grief, past the old need
to try to live like any minute an answer
is coming like mail. Something else is important now.

They come upon it never looking up from the music.

Dizzy Gillespie at the Blue Note

Somebody sat on his trumpet in 1953
and he's been playing with a bent bell
ever since.
               —*The New Yorker*

I will take you with me, I will
lift you the black balloons of his foreface
seem to say. And he does. Tosses you

like an infant, the whole exchange
having taken Time, a second child,
and tossed it too toward whatever Heaven

the bent bell sends an impossible music.
Just to flower like that, once,
and go again among strangers, knowing

not only what this jazz is besides black
history blonde white women sway to
but that Beauty displaces us. Bent

as if receiving other, more universally
pained sets of notes or tones,
the bell of the horn burgeons, gilt bloom

of some hope of anything like satisfaction
or even a momentary letting up of longing.
Be thankful there is no music encompassing

the one darkness makes babes of us all.
Be glad there are those so filled
to bursting that their jowl muscles weaken

and they blow it out, changed, pure.
How does this work? He owns the notes,
they cry to be loosed, he holds them forever.

31

The Laws of Salvage

This far down
Blacker latitudes lay claim. Divers,
In the bright custody of machine,
Under tremendous pressures, sift seabottom
For the ballroom loot loosed and gone.

Laws of salvage will not hold.
This much light dictates that what finishes here
May be mined: sea coal, blind, schooling fish,
Near righted lengths of hull, a safe
Settled on the broken shelf.

Where it is close and currentless, one
Ten billionth of the history of loss
Is up for grabs. These who come
Fear neither angel nor needling nitrogen
And descend through each and fluorescence

Equally. Outbreathed surface air, arc-lighted,
Figure-eights famously overhead. Being human,
To pass through is to open wounds, any entry
Its own new violation. Deep in the wreck,
Radio transmitting ambiguously of a need not to surface,

The divers cut power. Here, where passenger
And captain held to that foot or two of heaven
Itself going under,
There are bottles, upright,
In ghostly, undisturbed rows. Deckplates read:

TO STATEROOMS. There are stairs.
What is not changed or darkness enlists darkness.
Midships, a silence fixes the divers. In self-defense,
For the dead, they play a tape of Miles Davis.
Two skies down there is jazz.

Notwithstanding a Love of the Truth Instilled in Her by Her Father

Nothing fixes the light like dogwoods.
The very air tonight opals in high-beams.

Where she's been, a brickish colored rooster
crowed from a slanting yard's sheer drop-off.
The windows of the house were open
and rooster notes came in like dark water.
A breath of nightwind combed the hair
of draperies. The man she'd kissed, going,
said he'd never built a fire and it April.

The only kind of bed worth lying in
can't say what's taken place,
but this woman weeps again at the moon
setting in the silver curve of a car's fender,
tears ungathering at firstlight's floating
through the car, making the thing a wing of light.

What can't be saved is everywhere.
Successive cloudburst sweeps move slowly off.

She's going home to her husband.
She knows what it's like
to take ashes in her hands:
it's a gray flour, a white one then,
but it dusts and gets into everything.

Blue Gardens

These moments by Arby's swing 'round midnight
in the blue tube light glow of a Sohio car wash.
The car wash stays open all night year-round

so the end of the century can come on clean wheels.
In the strip mall between Arby's and the car wash
is a lopped-off loop of plum trees. Amazingly,

there are plums that tender full evening
a flesh of light like the faces in the cars.
Men in work clothes and Arsenio haircuts

call to one another over the roar, their voices
spilling away like wind or a boom box
playing Thelonius Monk endlessly. The car wash

fills with talk between cars, a towel man's
swearing that Miles Davis had his trumpet and case
blessed by the daughter of a mambo queen.

Huge night is here layered in blue, lifted up.
You think I think this is some kind of heaven of jazz,
don't you? I don't. I think it's "Monk's Mood"

talked over in the drying bay of a Sohio car wash.
I do think his music rises out of bad Sears speakers,
even the blue tube light adding a note.

These Fields

If the jacketed man on the 9600 John Deere
sees the LTD broken down at roadside,
if he feels the shock as a cold night wind
enters at the edges of a big, roving eye
of tractorlight, he doesn't show it.
The corn-head of the harvester goes gold
with droughted stubble given up
to the undercurrent of the cutting.
In a lit house by the road, one uncurtained
window is World Series baseball: Chili Davis
swings at a breaking ball, singles easily
on an error. The harvester driver
misses this, the spew of stubble and leaf
whirring out of the auger neck, filling
trailer after trailer. It must count
for something that the day ends as it began,
this the only game in town. When the driver
turns, there's a grinding of metal-on-metal
from beneath the tongue of the loader hitch.
It sounds all the way to the blue creek, the house,
to the road where the stalled LTD
gathers its last breath in a backfire.
A tow truck driver's radio's crying baseball,
Ford trucks, Bud Light. Everybody's driven by
these fields. Everybody's been this caught up
in labor of some kind or another. Who
hasn't seen the Hunter's Moon
unroll across the heavier light of machines,
the one light swelling? One stops like this
along a county road, good engine idling
in a salute to, what else, the work of our hands.

II

The ferryman must have taken the picture.

—Eudora Welty

Coal Island

The rivers in this southern state
want to cover everything—the pure fire
of a light on in a house at night,
the light visible through sycamores,
another unrecoverable December's end
lapping at marsh grass, something
about a place and all its histories
edging off the water's wearing at itself,
at the dull hour and the little light.

They rose, they fed stoves, they ate,
they went about the business-gone-bad-gone-good
of living stubbornly if not well—
there beyond that breast of limestone
the run-off of generations barely eroded.
If there's speaking, it's the falling free
of this bank, a big breath of river.

Letcher County, Kentucky

An hour before dawn in the coal towns in late summer
lights in the similar houses eclipse
the simple, locked-in hovering of one more day.
In the lane: rain crow, intervals of silence
and cricket singing. At this hour
the world sags. Gods and heroes, the rules
of the game bend, the more ambitious
having fenced woods and creek, private tunnels
of death-in-life. All turned or turning
to boxcars heaped black, hard extended curving lines,
an appetite for heat and night's lessening.

When coal was king they came here dreaming.
Now, Goose Creek runs rust-red when it runs.
Killdeer seining on the wing eat nothing
in the tender fashion indigenous these days.
Underground fires near Norton, on the Virginia side,
have smoldered thirty years—a stingy, continuous burn
raveling a deeper, unmoored darkness thread
by ragged thread. And all the deaths

in quiet houses—if there is Paradise, after,
we people it: Bill Barnett, going forever
after the same one loaf of bread
leading from Elkhorn Coal to four years in the Navy,
sons Doug and Billy at light's edge
in the same dark, forgiving God, forgiven,
no heaven apart from these lesser evidences of grace.

Yet in some cerebral folding or chemical recess
we know—in the way rock holds, in the way it's all
work—if hope were coal seams we'd mine willingly.
As it is, we buy big-kneed Joyce Yontz a print dress,
take it to her, drunk already.
If she's laughing, drunk herself, all the better.

Giants

for Jack Wright

Martin and Anna Bates, new-married, ease legs-first
to the feather-bedded floor of a wagon. Martin,
seven foot two and a half inches, in Anna's big arms,
pictures crews of Irish and Welsh felling miles of two-span
beech poplar maple, whole ancient-timbered sections
of Letcher County, Kentucky. Anna, seven foot five inches,
beside him, pregnant, has asked he not mention going home.
She too remembers, says the circus is food and a future
for two so accustomed to stares. He opens the twelve-pound
pocket watch, wrought gold gift of Victoria,
Queen of Great Britain, Empress of India.
In the still night on Hampshire Down, Martin Bates,
sideshow attraction, hears a mill wheel turn and take water.

———————

Rain pops for hours on the canvas, lakes of it leveed
and exploding levees. Near morning, after making love,
Martin remarks how his son or daughter should know
the simple ring and return of fiddle music,
how joy, like a whiskey, begins at a boil in the mountains.

———————

There are ways there and back
the trigonometries of which resolve quietly, luminously
into the ability to bear the weight of the going.
Ships in open sea, in approaching storm,
intuit angels of ice and wind and spoiling wave,
courses put across at precisely the moment
when what is summonable is outline and foreign.
Mid-ocean, cupped hands of companionable light resist charting.
The trusted sextant sights and resights,

being all the equipment of habit that works.
And what of firm soil after undulating months at sea,
landed horizonline so finite and abruptly vertical
as to make of the slow extendings of continents
something dreamed? The world ashore censed
with high lappings, bay breezes that track and sweep us,
spilling news of essential things: cramped trains
of immigrant and native crossing insular slopes,
level miles of trestled valley. In one lighted traincar,
a man takes the gloved hands of a large woman, uncovers
and kisses them, equally.

———————

In a log house by the thawing north fork of the Kentucky River,
Anna Bates has just pushed out the largest live birth
in recorded history. Twenty-three pounds eleven ounces.
Bruised, it breathes, follows Martin's watch.
When it dies near evening, unnamed, Anna will kiss
and wrap a brooding likeness, famous body purchased by wire
by a health museum in Cleveland, Ohio,
where, in a white room, behind glass, suspended,
it is the shadowed face of Elkhorn Creek, Pound Gap,
the Cumberlands. *Look at me*, it says. *For one day,
in one high-ceilinged room, I was all the fire.*

On Horseback D.V. Bentley Carries Home News
and Something More

Pine groves and a beeyard either side of Neon-Hemphill Road
accept snow, swaths of serviceable shadow, anything
a man on horseback might happen on at this hour.
The saddled mare, as though she too believes in greater good,
unasked, noses homeward, this man she carries
buying Neon, Kentucky, a kindness at a time, doctoring
Potter Wright MacFall Collier Caudill Bentley Harlow,
arm-patting, mixing poltice, cutting natal cord.
Between jolts, dozing, he dreams again turn-of-the-century
Hopkin's House, Nashville, a manacled Harry Houdini.
Standing room only, caped assistant: *I draw the curtain so.*

On arriving, exhausted, he calls up to the house, waits
to be cut from encased stirrups, ice freight jettisoned
the way the angel ghost demon was that night above Rock House.

———————

They say that for centuries this was cursed ground,
nations of Indians agreeing, in accordance with legend,
to make no permanent claim on the land. Muscled bands
of men and boys, wide-roaming, must have aimed arrows
at elk deer bear, spirit-gifts in the hills beyond.
Abed with spinal meningitis, near death,
Doc Bentley retraces repeatedly his ride from Hemphill
the night he felt a form drop gently into the saddle behind.
At the entrance to Elkhorn Coal, hill and road ahead
darkened suddenly.

———————

Having quarried the first granite for building
in Letcher County—this much for a drugstore-barbershop-
hotel, this for a bank—D.V. Bentley takes stock.

43

Not so much to bask in long-houred days, the sweat of men,
as knowing he is less alone, more approved of
for having masterminded the labor in just this way.

At the road, hip flask and well water celebration commenced,
Lester Wright Tom Collier Sam T. lead the backslapping,
cut stone piled earth pre-history flaring, angular,
thoroughly admired, higher up.

When the cups have been around, Sam T., barrel-built,
suspendered, begins a shuffle in the dust.
Little clouds at his feet boil and rise, D.V. handclapping,
calling encouragement as if all Kentucky, all ambition,
stood absolutely still, twenty or so men
glad in that last hour of light when tiredness,
like a creek, any wind in the oaks, sounds by the road.

The Edge of Heaven

for Inez

There is a meagerness to hills in eastern Kentucky
in May, a wealth of laurel thickets starved brilliant,
ineradicable. Above Hemphill mine-fouled Little Creek
laps at andiron, truck tire, stove-by-the-road.
Earl Potter is walking, Zane Grey paperback
in a pants pocket, one ten-dollar bill and a thirst
for company. The fact he's spent a year and a month
in Ashland Penitentiary for a barfight in India,
was court-martialed, hurts his reputation not at all.
Married now, a miner, he knows well the hard incline
of the lane and a half from Potter Town to the Fountain
and ten booths, barstools, a jukebox and upright fan.
Johnny Belcher, guard for the Fountain,
stands a head taller than Earl and is as afraid
of the Potters as he is Earl's black Shepherd dog, Snowball:

Pack a lunch you fight a Potter. In the Fountain,
careless, Earl lets his mouth and watered whiskey
guide him, idiot hands, into trouble.
Just like that: shot and amazed, supporting himself
on the arms of men who will survive to repeat the *Oh, God
That sonofabitch* tomorrow in the changing house.

———————

Having heard the news, Bill Potter and R.B. Hall
go to Johnny Belcher's. It is light yet,
the fifth of Early Times nearly empty.
Where the trees have been lumbered out, sumac starts
rise between stump and silence it takes a hundred years
to grow into. The dynamite, blunted, sufficient,
nestles in R.B.'s veined hands. "Here," he says.
It will be simple: sheathed seditiously at each corner,

45

one in the window, *personal-like*.
Blow the leaves off beech and poplar half a mile
down the hollow. Get his children too. Wife.
Every goddamn chicken and dog here to the ridge
where .22 pistols made a song of pop bottles
summers they learned better than kill for sport or practice.
At the house, a door opens. One big-eared, bibbed-
overalled boy of nine or ten jettisons dishwater
in a spray, sweeps a landing, goes in.

———————

On a road from Neon
Bill Potter recalls his mother's vision, how she prayed
and fasted, rocked and sang that her dead son
might, if not in this life then after,
receive some dispensation toward mercy.
A day and a night, a day, wailing
until what business anyway has a Great White Heron
descending on a ruined lawn above Goose Creek.
What business indeed at the dusk edge of Heaven
except to say that if not each whimper among cries
then one cry, this. Wings extending,
even the throes of pre-flight must have seemed holy.
And when it rose again, circled the lighted houses
of Kentucky, beat its shadowed way through the air,
it was soul went up, silly, inarticulate histories
we would explode were the right man home.

Field of Stone

...but they're our dead
and our sick, and we will slake their lips
with our very hearts if we must, and we must.

—William Matthews

The night Willis Collier's daughter Frances
tethered bedsheets to the iron of her headboard
and climbed a story and a half down to dance all night,
she paid. Pregnant and Frances Potter before fall,
all bound and life beginning.

———————

Frank Potter, Justice of the Peace, widower, had ten children.
He politicked nights; like Frances, did what was needed,
required. When Doc Bentley told him, explained how far along,
he thanked him, counted out bills.
It was a goodly walk to Willis Collier's, sun shining.

———————

Old Regular Baptist hymns are "lined out": a man or woman
stands at the front and repeats, before it is sung,
the next line. No hymnals, the song, spoken quickly,
is taken up, without instrumentation.
Ionce waslost butnow amfound
I-igh wa-unce wa-uz lost bu-ut na-ow am found...

Evenings, she'd talk-sing this way until I feigned sleep.
Even that might not do it. And if I stirred,
stories of shootings and lives cut short
would worry me into the warm crook of her arm and middle,
small huddle of boy and fear and happiness at being held.

———————

The difference between my mother and her
was cause for shouting on occasion. I'd hear them
in the hall of the house in Kettering, swearing.
At issue, the fact my mother, recently divorced,
working full-time, needed help. My mother, slight,

a smoker, could shout *Then leave, goddamit*
with such resonant hate you knew it was an ugly world
and sad, really. The summer afternoon my mother slapped
my father with a sandal, blistered his face
for bringing me home in the same car as the woman
he was seeing, my grandmother took a blow to the shoulder.
Though I recall clearly that it was my father,
defending himself, who hit her, she swore my mother

struck her. *A-purpose*, she told the Kettering Police
who dutifully wrote it down.

_____

Every so often, regardless, she'd return home.
Something about residency requirements, a pension.
One trip, crossing the Ohio, the great aching black
made me ask what happens when we die. In the dark,
honed blade of her nose reflected in the curved
glass of the Greyhound, she said pray, said
Jesus knew well enough where Kentucky was.

_____

Graveside, Pentecostals and Old Regulars
war at song until the cumbrous music
is neither simply joyless nor droning
but an explanation of long trial and little triumph.
Her work, done well or poorly, ends now,
eighty years of it and a dream of resurrection.
The brief girl of her, petty mother,

the lie of faith that is truth finally by default.
Entirely ours, she settles against old flesh sacks,
slack ropes of bone, closed eyes. For all her rage,
one rose, specific and small-leaved across her.

Beyond, in a field, men and boys stack brush and rot.
Night eddies about, smoke and light
spiring, quarrelling aloft.

1954

Palmate leaves the color of cinnamon fan down,
heave nakedness and change, nothing and everything,
onto roadway. Two lives, little whirlwinds,
share the long drive, Dayton to Neon,
new son bawling with colic.

A year from artillery shortfalls, menacing cold,
a divorce, Roy Bentley's father, Roy Bentley,
grips the wheel of the '50 Chevy Bel-aire, hums
Hank Williams. When they stop for trains
or traffic, for towns,
Nettie Bentley lights a cigarette, hands him
the pack and matches. They sit, smoking,
the boy feeding, waking into news of H-bombs, Sinatra.

Gray banks of trees rub horizon, maneuver
pools of sky into cramped bands,
latitudes of dusk at noon. The light,
diminished, carries coal smoke and solitudes,
sediments of dreamed love, pre-sleep.
What liveliness survives bounds in bodies of deer,
the rest moving in decline, anesthetized.

What they wish for is ease, warmth.
What they are entitled to is memory, beginnings
sharp and certain, present futures
in error unlearned, lost, heard in leaffall.

The Picture My Father Promised

A true story. Ever since my father
brought home the black oak framed
faces of Quiller and Ellen Bentley,
my sadly human, homely even, great-
grandparents, I listened with interest

to the halftruths of our family history.
The picture had been tinted
in a way that made Quiller and Ellen
appear made-up, nineteenth century.
I can't tell from the photograph

what either of them thought of this life,
but my father becomes noticeably sad
then strangely buoyant when he speaks
of the picture or his boyhood. As if
the fact his mother went berserk

and had to be institutionalized
soon after his birth, says nothing
of the love in these two faces.
These are the two who locked his mother
in an upstairs room on learning

of her pregnancy by a married man.
Who first shuttled her off
to the sanitarium in Lexington
when all she really was was angry.
My father knows this. Knows I know.

He knew the afternoon he promised the picture
and all the ambiguity attending it.
We used to have to take his mother
back to Kentucky and the sanitarium.
She used to sit in the backseat

of our '48 Mercury—aloof, a shadow
passing across her face before the anger
broke in waves and she called me
"little son-of-a-bitch" out of the blue.
It was always nightfall

when we left her, always evening
and hard to read my father's face
on the drive home to Ohio. The light
from the dashboard subtracted everything
except his eyes, and even they glowed

with a light not of this world or the next
but some distant huddling together at last,
all our deaths and lives turned to one life
we fall through, the only warmth
handed over in a dark car.

Red Jaguar

At one hundred forty miles an hour, more,
something's about to break or really hum.
That sound sweeps us along, heat-struck,
beyond billboards, the local world's
separation of church and highway.
It's Sunday. He's doing work on a friend's car.
I'm a kid, I think. *I can't die.*
I prayed once with the television, I've
petted Rin Tin Tin. The Jaguar breaks right
to the four-four time of a Dayton AM station.

We're talking a deeply lacquered rouge-red.
He's planted at the wheel, my father.
He looks like he's choosing life for us
at every turn, slippery-curved life-or-death
hiding in the XKE's hot brakes. I'm eight.
It's about three-thirty in the afternoon.
Heat from the long hood rises in waves.

He's smiling. "What's wrong, Buck?"
The sides of his flat-top haircut are sunlight,
angular. Once I watched him at his Shell station,
washing the blind body of the Jaguar
in the tube-lit neon of his name. I saw him
open an arm on some under-steel. Blood
and soap suds raced down a gutter, carrying
his love for the facts of cars, fast cars.

There's an Elvis movie on a drive-in marquee.
Big acrylic letters blow by like black leaves.
It's rained. We both shiver, the top down.
Water shows on the road, sheets of water
blousing from the windshield and wings, coming in,

the sea-sound of rain in the tires, one note,
radio talk become the noise of gravel shoulder
and the car's grabbing for anything to hold on to.

Like God or George Jones, I'm along for the ride.
And when he leans forward to shift, one-
handing the simply matter of the wheel,
maybe I'm driving. Maybe there's a valley
misting after rainfall, and distances
greater than the reach of roads.

The Love of the Long Married

You know how it is: their nakedness,
no mystery, steeps like a tea.
She wants only to forget and so
has drawn a bath. He is trying so hard
to cross a sea of dailiness, another
of indifference. It should have been otherwise.
They were practical and survived
the various deaths, stitched of their lives
together a modest quilt that nearly covered.
Kiss me, she says. And he does.
First a scent then everything sweet
sighted along a thigh. It's summer, late.
Long, uncurtained windows open onto starlight's
tendency to ribbon in a downpour.

The Orchard the Dry Year

*And yet if it's true, as I've read
that the starving body eats itself,
it's true it eats the heart last.*

— Katha Pollitt

In an orchard once
Bobby Ramsdail and I learned to wait.
Sisters, our mothers had moved in together:
their husbands, our fathers, gone.
His, in a Sidney jail; mine
off somewhere, remarried.
By July we'd taken to climbing
to the brown centers of trees,
wearying old oak and apple
with looking out onto the drab, flat
tabletop of Dayton, Ohio.
Any higher meant risking dry upper limbs.

George Kosta, oldest boy on the block at 13,
taught us how drought works, how
every so often it forgets to rain.
Till someone reminds it. Bobby and I,
drawn in, trusting,
asked instructions. *Indians stripped,
danced stark naked by fires. You could
probably get by with streetlights, maybe
underwear.*
           Not cruelly, I laugh now
when Bobby writes he is unhappy.
In a card I remind him of the dance—
hard, lanky bodies moving at midnight
in the middle of Comanche Drive, highest point
in Kettering—how a better vision
might have waited rain the way we did
our fathers: Bobby's, released in the fall;

mine, home in a year, two.
Our way we had another counting
that whole month, hope,
though after each tucking in
we watched from the top bunk
the day's dry going, that hollowing,
dark to darker. The happy night
it rained, apple boughs let down
and spilled a poor failed fruit,
loose branching, the story of our lives.

Now, my cousin
who I love like a brother
phones in the night, says he'll
see me soon, that he is taking
antidepressant drugs, Lithium.
I might cry some, he says. *Don't mind it.*

Times of Day

Eat it; and you will taste more than the fruit:
The blossom, too,
The sun, the air, the darkness at the root.
—Louise Brogan

I swam that whole summer
at the Boys' Club in Dayton, Ohio.
Indoors and naked, hundreds of us,
Yankees baseball on the public address,
Roger Maris chasing Ruth's
single season home run record.
I was seven and didn't follow baseball.
The water was cold
and shriveled small penises
even smaller.

Older boys, easily ecstatic,
drew long breaths
and followed each other, blindly,
down from the high dive.
On his way, one passed and spoke
conspiratorially
of fingerfucking, petty theft.
What else was there to do
but go headfirst in, with the others,
then, surfacing,
find that anonymity of flesh
among flesh? This body neither innocent
nor frightened, just new.

One boy who had no arms
showed me the harness of his hooks,
said he'd drown even in the shallows
and I believed him. Out of water
he recited baseball statistics,
said Ford Frick said Maris

had to get the record
in the same number games.
He'll do it, he said. *He's got to.*

———————

You are you're mother, he says,
drives on toward Dayton,
drunk, in the rain.
I pray it will end, cinch hard
the seat belt he will say he tightened
when the big car left the road.

It is possible he reached across, my father,
missed the belt, is another now
and trims his trees to the bone.
No mess from fruit or leaves, small reward
to watch them bend so in summer.
I miss the younger man, who risked his life
and mine, took that tight curve
at close to 100, in a thunderstorm.

He would say he is little changed,
that what I call epiphanies
fall in upon themselves and two histories,
nothing gained. I would argue
that he bled, remind him of it.
Besides, the rain was real:
we climbed from the wreck
into it, were roused by the chill of it.

All day he continues at the trees,
subtracting,
hauling down limbs, burning.

———————

This year waxwings descend early,
lapsed meadow gold with coltsfoot.
Not home, not half way there,
hundreds of tufted heads turn, alert.
For an hour, two,
then even the far shore will not do,
long green long brown reverse
of oaks in water, Y of light.

We are the locals.
We know the times of day
the lake will be peopled
and when to park and kiss winter on.
The paved places and soft,
little stores on the way in
and what they stock, hours to avoid town.

                        South of here
my great-grandfather, Quiller Bentley,
burned to death in a field fire.
They were clearing winter grasses.
The wind changed, shifted,
and he was caught, walled in.
I imagine that interval
before flame reached across.
One life not enough, not nearly.

                        The trees go dark.
A man passes a fresh-rolled cigarette
across the hood of Chevy
the color of cayenne.

Lighted Jesus

In the offices, doors open,
a floor-to-ceiling Dolores Del Rio
contends with a lighted Jesus
for a chance to entice passersby
with that overstatement of faith
in the black-and-white simplicities of lives
in no way simple. A nursing instructor
comments, wants to know, by title and year,
if she's seen all her movies.
"I never liked her, *politically*," she says,
"but she made you forget."
The same woman later the same day
wants to know why my wife
lives seventy miles distant, why,
in all the pictures of family on all the shelves,
she is absent. As if affection
means having at least one overcalmed moment
of closeness or pure self enframed, lighted.
I change the subject, consider instead
a great-uncle, D.V. Bentley, a doctor
who owned a town in Kentucky
and, depending upon whom you believe,
kept a mistress so privately
his wife and the woman could pass in the drugstore
without incident, eyes meeting in secret affirmation
that, mindful always of consequence, we make
and bend and become those rules we assent to.
I remember the shark scene in *Bird of Paradise*,
Dolores Del Rio crossing oceans of culture
to free the White Hero/Joel McCrea from certain
and terrible death, later the night-swim-kiss-
on-a-bed-of-roses wedding dance, Dolores
swaying, all navel and 1932 nearly-topless.
That ready, unaffected smile Joel McCrea
walked through fire and volcano curse for.

Of course when the volcano blew, the Hero,
bound beside Dolores, recited the Lord's Prayer,
asked the One God, his, for deliverance.
And when it came, in the form of her life for his,
it was as Christian a gesture as D.V. Bentley
acknowledging, in the morally superior climate
of 1950's America, his mistress in his will.
Perhaps he'd seen dark-haired Dolores Del Rio
in headdress, stepping to the burst rim
of the volcano, to appeasement.
Perhaps he was awash in the knowledge
that there are those who waste not a single
bright ounce of this life.
All things being equal, he was saying,
from any blue-watered heaven, clearly,
you can walk to hell.

White Cadillac

They're almost gone, whose chrome-
nosed front-ends took that generation
born into the Great Depression, started them
sleekly down roads brimmed with no rest
from wanting, living well the new Jesus.
My father had one—a '53 Eldorado
with the wraparound windshield, gas cap
in the rear taillight: a wire-wheeled,
white-sidewalled open boat of a car.
A pretty sight those blunted curves
celebrating victories in war, what we have
after pulling out all the stops.
By the pool, he reminds me my short-stick
child fingers brushed the floor fan
under the passenger-side front seat, says
it took two bar towels to stop the bleeding.
There are moments waiting to be stumbled
into like a car. He turns into himself,
sighs, drains a glass, says he'd have had
those leather bench seats re-upholstered
in red if he'd had any sense. For a moment
I see what's for sale in the *Playboy* ad
for the Franklin Mint's 1/24th scale model
of that first Eldorado—for the most part
it's his journey, theirs: receiving
without a thought the blessings of linear time
and a factory job. Hell, with 210 horsepower
V-8's, even Death has to bust ass
to come even and call, Pull over, goddammit.
I want to buy the model for him, the metal
of steel-as-memory afloat in the Florida air.
Years ago, you can almost hear him,
the fear-of-fear swollen words moving us

back momentarily—you can love this place—
to a showroom reeking of the scent of tires,
the transaction his smudged photograph
of a life not unhappy though not blue-
fountained, something wonderfully made,
flung at loss and in praise of vent
windows, coupe doors, moonlight-on-chrome.

Tobacco Barns

It's October. The black, slatted sides
of the tobacco barns along State Route 8
are open, summer's turned leaf hanging in rows
the color of cut cedar. Elvis is on the radio,
"I Can't Help Falling in Love with You".
It's misting, and this much of the Ohio River
has white caps breaking before and after
great forever-going barges. Driving,

I'm on my way to hear Gurney Norman
give a talk on regionalism. What I want
is to hear anyone from Letcher County
who's kept his accent say the place names
I grew up with: *Whitesburg Hazard Neon.*
I need to hear them. I'm reading
a handwritten map taken down over the phone
in a badly lit room at the Daniel Boone Motor Inn.

A pair of turned sycamores by the gravel lot
of Augusta High School send down leaves
the size of a man's hand. One leaf has caught
and spins on the antenna of a Ford truck; several
have landed in the truck bed. The leaves
aren't the color of tobacco in October, but it's close.
I go in. There's a date in a crest above the stage
of a gymnasium-auditorium: 1926. Gurney's

moving around the gym, circumnavigating
a raised platform and half-circle of folding chairs.
He looks rested. Like maybe he slept somewhere
besides the Motor Inn across the river in Aberdeen.
He's in a windbreaker, he's grayed some
since I saw him, and he shakes my hand
like he means it. He's got a smile going like a fire,
takes me in and I'm warmed, truly.

Afterwards, I'm driving the road along the river.
The tobacco barns are still there, still open.
The white caps on the Ohio have turned golden
in late day sun, a speedboat splitting them
to Maysville. On the radio, Don Williams.
I know the song and howl the whole way,
my voice becoming every poor sonofabitch
who has missed the light on tobacco barns.

III

His body was so small. The rage was pathetic but its pitifulness was unfair. If he had been stronger, he could have done something. And even so, as he churned along the trail behind the men there was something different in him, something more impressive. For these few minutes he was not afraid of the men.

—Norman Mailer. *The Naked and the Dead.*

Any One Man

Here they have your shaved chest open
and the bleeders clamped off
nonchalantly. Here the trouble is
the wall clock says you've been like this—
draped, motionless on the stage of a table,
your tired heart's blue-veined tethers
restitched for the better part of six hours—
until they're ready to call it.
All that's flashing is an occasional bolt
of superimposed brilliance going off
on the instruments, abstract crosses of light.
Of course they've tried shocking the thing.
The surgeon in charge, one arm a deep
root in the chest, waits.
For an idea, any, to take your life's cadence
from behind Death's aquarium's thick glass
and put it back at home in this world
of the next in-filling EKG blip and crest.
An intern you said you'd wear your kilt for
asks can she take a turn. There's
a wide sweeping motion to the hand
as it goes in, the arc of the love for any
one man that second and successive try
at steady compressions. Whatever you're thinking—
Wish to hell I'd jogged more. God,
how lonely and cold I am—you're
in a face-off with your own body.
See, they're saying, there's no point
going on like this. He's any man
dreaming of a fall he can't wake from.
Here, I'm left-handed. It's not that late.

The Heart Has Its Reasons

The night I witness the arrests, fires burn.
Policia round up *campesinos*.
The men move without talking.
The wall where they stop

has wide, white marks at intervals
to help the young *soldados* aim.
The *soldados* cannot see so well in the dark and rain,
but if they hit something

the *teniente* will finish it.
For this, the heart has its reasons,
splashes of moral sweetness, platitudes,
hoarse whisper of hate so hot it phosphoresces.

In the headlamps' hard staring, commands.
The little caves of the chest wait.

A Place to Come Back to

It's a shame about your friend and the others
who are innocent and being held. But they are
Americans, and that is enough.
> —Iranian diplomat in an interview
> on *All Things Considered*

All day it has rained choruses of cicadas
keeping appointments, haggling in the light
and silences under eaves between storms.
There is rain in the haunting, purposeful

voice-over on the video tape, the slow
rotation of the hanged body of a Marine
lieutenant colonel, damp heat of Beirut
clinging to the contours of his new sleep

like a uniform. Rain's forced singing
is in the black blindfold, the blue
braid of cord strung between roof rafter
and the held breath become the noose.

The blood-bruise of wrist bindings, these
too solid truths float like dust-motes
in the light of witnesses clad
in camouflage, T-shirts, x's of ammunition.

These too become rain, radiating thunder.
The terrible indications of a flood
of talk of countries we have loved,
and love. Next thing we know,

the deluge, in a sort of game of futures,
has turned out the lethargy in the summer air.
Soon the cicadas will sing. Of other deaths
scouring the continents of other afternoons.

A Swim before Dying

Finally Mother called in another doctor.
He was equally well known, but he was in
high disrepute. He was thought to be on
drugs, and he probably was. His behavior
was quite eccentric: he was known to slap
his patients around on occasion.
                    —John Huston. *An Open Book*

The spillway, pulsing and slacking off,
opened on the hour. Everything moved
blindly forward, boiled toward midsummer's
rush past standing shells of chestnut trees
dead on banks abutting alfalfa fields.

The re-immersion was what you wanted.
Not to efface evening's diffuse light
nor plane down into darkness
but glide into that life behind the eyes,
an endless getting on with it.

A sleeve of starred water rocked you,
ungently bore you center-stream: weight
of low, steady breathing birthed
in the year of the fire horse. They said
your heart was bad, congenitally weak

and could only surprise them
by seeing you to Labor Day. What joy
to drown the best educated guesses,
flatten that Irish flesh
like a constellation defiantly come loose

from its slice of sky, all of it
so American you could only rise
out of the worst could happen, the rest

an immense, live thing hauling the least
and best up from some weave of soul,
out once more into the air. The world
and its named rivers riding it too,
caught in undercurrents worthy of you.
A night later, to do it again.

Rowing in Eden

In the eternities between hours,
he began a boat. Of course his hands
rebelled, betrayed him, and every tool
took forever to carve or foreshorten.
Before Eve, before the Tree.

God could have been at hand
but then He wouldn't have been God.
Already His long reach left the world
to be made over, improvised.
Had he waited for blind faith to fell

the bur oak, the herd of unnamed animals
that turned at the noise
would have continued on.   The silence
after would have been the leaves
unstirred by that first stubborn fall

through new air ballasted with first death.
The idea of the boat had been effort enough:
Something in the rocking of leaves on water...
Something in the rift between amazements...
Had it come later, they'd have credited

the woman. As it was, it was all his.
The wrecks of the early hulls
became Memory, the untended stuff
to row to and from on the lake.
The lake, banked by nectaries abloom

in perpetual midsummer, accepted the slow
motions of a man rowing tentatively at dusk.
Soon, so much of him lived in the pulling
of the oars that songs commenced. He sang
of other leaf-shades, of dreamed lakes.

Somewhere in the singing it occurred to him
to call out. To God, immured in shadow.
Unacquainted with the sound, God,
up from sleep, heard the burden
in the labor of the tongue, the need

and not the absolute beauty in mirroring
one likeness in the lake of another.
What to do? How to answer?
It must have taken consideration
of the long, intimate act of rowing:

the synchronies of fist, of beating heart
and blood and the pure, seasonless ecstasy
of rowing the light out and back,
intent on the isthmus Night makes, the finger-
toward-His-hand the boat is.

Roman Polanski's *Chinatown*

In the barber shop, an alley, information
is passed which leads to the moment,
knifeblade to the nose, when we learn
that resolve is what replaces innocence.

As Jake Gittes says, this business
requires a certain *finesse*, meaning,
after you've shown a man explicit pictures
of his wife and whomever, you tell him
to be careful driving home. All right,
you've been shot at, nearly drowned,
beaten, lost a perfectly good Florsheim shoe.

This is the life we make for ourselves
by allowing others to own the valleys
and water rights, orange groves, orchards.
Even the run-off drowns the disenfranchised,
or tries to, nightly in a flush of moonlight.

You're limping disgustedly away from
the mess of your life thus far. Later,
in your offices, a true fiction of a woman
whose whole straining composition
is reducible to a single strand of pearls
iridescent against silk, blue black mourning veil
moving with the little warm fronts of her breathing.

The woman lights a cigarette, one
already going in the ashtray beside her.
Smoke, rising, highlights a flaw
in the iris of her right eye. It's about
the lies she's telling, your not knowing
when, if ever, the truth-telling began.

The Baseball Wars

I think the affair—if that's
what it's been—is over when she
returns the Anais Nin and Miles Davis,
the lambskin condoms and Edgar Cayce
Aura & Glow massage oil.
The same day though, she calls
to remind me of a PBS special on Nicaragua.
While I have her on the phone:
Did you have to bring back the condoms?
"Larry has a vasectomy," she says, too proudly.
Then, because the way she feels about me
has been a secret, even to her:
"They were hard to explain."
That evening, Daniel Ortega on public broadcasting—
the presidential box at the Nicaraguan
baseball championships, AK-47 at his feet—
I recall an afternoon she and I
had gone to an arboretum, parked.
White Toyota grounds truck circling,
she'd joined an elect group
who'd had sex by the Japanese Garden
in the open in daylight. On the television
the interviewer asks the source
of the Nicaraguan love of baseball.
Ortega, blandly: "The US Marines."
It is all invasion, imperialisms of spirit
in which those who can
walk us to a rise, sun silhouetting
a stand of buckeyes, and speak eloquently
of the relationship between sex and closeness, love
and dying. I want to tell her
that her going is her right and fine,
that I will be better somehow
for having found her, lost her,

recovered estranged reserves of self
as if coming together and uncoupling
were mechanisms of succession.
She knows that whatever dark slide
I take from her is my motion
and part of the politics.
I want to tell her I have Daniel Ortega
recounting his first arrest and beating at 14,
a judge who would hear nothing
of the torture of children.
I'll be all right. Certain of us
know full well it's pain and sport
and all we know or ever will know.
If she'd stayed, there would have been
years, lifetimes of the stuff.
It's a small, simple world and what we do.

Marciano

The photographs in *Collier's*
  said he wanted to be liked. Sparring
   into the mirrors of the iron-lungs

on the men's polio wards. Visiting
  a leper colony where he stripped
   to the waist and shadow-boxed

for twelve hundred who chanted in Filipino:
God bless you, Rocky. May you reign long.
   Clowning with Ike, grandfather

to the nation: "So you're the heavyweight
  champion of the world. You know,
   somehow I thought you'd be bigger."

Towering over Jersey Joe Wolcott, a god
  down in the 13th round, on the ropes.
   Having a Coke with Allie Colombo,

an old friend, at a luncheonette in New York:
  a regular guy. So we liked him.
   So what if he could quote purses: *Louis*

*vs. Max Schmeling, second fight: $150,000
a minute.* So what if he only saw his
   wife, no Marilyn Monroe, four months a year.

So what if he was Roman Catholic and refused
  to box on Sunday. He was the Rock.
   In 3-D movies of the second Walcott fight,

the power in the right hand lifting
  Jersey Joe as it would any mortal, whole
    theaters of us in the glasses, transfixed,

by association ourselves undefeated.
  Our transient attentions
    were his, the burning focus

of millions who could no more deliver him
  from the sudden downward arc of his life
    than apologize

for the slow motion horror of its descent.
  What could we have done?
    No amount of clean money

pressed into powerful hands, no
  letters to Presidents, no slice of a once-
    and-future purse could tempt him.

The stalled plane, borne up
  as long as it was by fate, rocked,
    dropped like any tired fighter

through the cloud of his excuses.
  The lighted air went dark, the air
    surrounding him like ring ropes.

The Book of Boxing

Of course, there is no such book in print.
—Frank Deford

1

When Archie Moore was, as they said of him,
"39 going on 42," he sat Marciano down
in the second. The sweet physics

of the jab, the bebop choreography
of 129 knockouts. And *balls*—

kidding Tommy Wright, Moore's fugitive
father, on the occasion of their first
face to face meeting: *Say, Nigger,*
you know the po-lice is looking for you?

2

It is 1949. Toledo, Ohio.
Archie Moore has the Alabama Kid
in a neutral corner and is scoring.

The Kid, used up, small, moves
like something not at all deserving

of the word *human*. The "geometry
of how the body should be set when one

boxes" drops from him, a blood.

This round, the fourth,
they will give Moore the fight, the KO
coming on a right as earned

as the outline of a man staggering
under a weight he has carried forever
and would relinquish, gladly, at once,
were the weight anything but his life.

3

Of Marciano: *They said he was
a house wrecker, and he was,
but it took him a volley
to get the job done.* Of Yvon Derelle:

This guy: one punch.

Of Jimmy Bivins: *Caught me down
on my knees. But I made him pay for it.*

Neither in the short light of December
in Keokuk, Iowa, nor in Orange, New Jersey,
did Archie Moore ever—*ever*—take a dive.

Not even to some white hope
in some tank town where, "in them days,"
the black fighter might "lie down"
to sell tickets. Joey Maxim,

light heavyweight champion of the world
in 1952, learned it. Learned it again
in the rematch he lost to Moore in '54,
the year I was born.

4

In such-and-such city or town tonight
it is 1938. Archie Moore and Johnny

"Bandit" Romero, main eventers, wait the bell.
In the crowd a minor gangster
pours himself three, three and a half fingers
of Scotch from a hip flask. The ring

is awash in voices, light, the scalloped
shadows of the ropes. Men who pay good money
to see other men stand on the borders

between each time the train slows
and that stop where *The Book of Boxing* says

We have, each of us, nothing
We will give it to each other—these

call across collapsing rows of seats,
colorful banners of futility
rustling in dense, hovering smoke.

5
Whatever they're paying them,
any of us, it isn't enough.

Not in some more perfect world
or this one seen through illusions
an uppercut or good right hand
sends packing, scuttling back

across the little Harlems of memory.

If there were an alternate route
through countryside golden with day's
end, in another light or our own reflection

it would read backward and where, then,
would we look to slip the blows?

[for Howard McCord]

Trick of the Light

for Lee Martin

When finally you knew
  this much of your life
    was not to succeed, you emptied boxes

that had been filling steadily:
  anonymous echinoderm, tidal lapses,
    benign families

of striking, maillotted women,
  Hawaiian-shirted men
    with abundant stomachs,

the white-bordered language of keeping.
  It was the work you'd wanted, distracted
    from talk of needs, partnering,

an acuity in the majority of the stills—
  earned incompletion—
    though the pictures, little miracles

of conspiracy, aimed at fixity: a child's
  wash of footprints, bleached citizenries
    of shell unbuilding ocean

in that breakdown that might have
  but didn't inform, washed-up man-of-war
    putrifying

on sand that had seen and forgotten
  and seen worse so often
    that larger pressings at tragedy

had fallen easily away, unpleasantnesses.
  And so she left, having marshaled
    sufficient contempt to steel her.

For weeks you'd worked in the dim,
   abandoned, middle distances of the prints
      muddied—various exposures and papers

experiments at impossible extremes.
   When you'd come up, to eat or sleep,
      to the boxes,

it had been as if disgust
   had stepped aside on the stairs. The house,
      the foyer at evening as bare and strange

as watching oneself move
   haltingly through wreckage, any
      of a thousand failed photographs

pirated, boarded by poor composition,
   imbalance, bad sky—
      some accident or angle

or trick of the light. It might tease
   for years, winking at sturdy faith.
      Still, you'd seen the perfect

metaphor for it in tides. Waves
   were warm, encircling, memorized you.
      You could call the going-out

love, for all the good it would do.

Everyone Says So Who Claims to Know the Story

*Disposables are great for a fast blast, but they
aren't for everyday use. Less finely honed than
regular needles, they have tiny burrs that hurt
like hell and tear up your veins.*
        —Albert Goldman. *Ladies & Gentlemen, Lenny Bruce*

It's February, winter in New York.
Lenny Bruce, *Leonard Alfred Schneider,*
in a room at the America, right arm ruined,
searches the small of his knee for a vein.
In more than the usual grey below, old Sears furnace
forces heat, sporadically, rhythmically, upward.
On a television, Dorothy Gale, dreaming of Kansas,
dances a reel with Scarecrow and Tin Man, technicolor Oz
reduced to black-and-white, commercials.
Needle in, Lenny lets blood and methedrine mix
in the chamber, then *zoom.* Kissing God, he calls it.
He is making thirty-five hundred a week.
The desk clerk, long distance operator, maid and maitre d',
call him Mister. In hip rebellion, he knows the first names
of pimps, embraces hit men; in hip confusion,
is building a house in the Hollywood hills. Sammy Davis
complains how difficult it is to get a table stageside.
Today, on the dresser, kitchen matches, disposable syringe,
a book his daughter made. The book, the sort
endemic to children: maverick letters, names aslant,
frenzied color. Even the stapling, love's amateur spiel.
Second generation immigrant, schooled on Times Square
freak shows—Professor Roy Heckler and His Flying Flea Circus,
lady with the enema tubes, human balloon—
he understands playing to the room, when not to.
In Philly once to perform for Rotarians, a convention,
one of the audience said something disparaging about Jews.
Lenny: *The lecture today: the Benefits of Circumcision,*
and unzipped his Levis, pissed.

In the America, he is taping boxed ampules high up
in a fireplace draw, stashing. The ancient furnace churns.
On the screen, flowering seas of poppies reach, dark,
whole bedded, fevered world nodding.

View from the Great Southern Hotel

Couples entwined, couples
not entirely together,

dark men and white
all manner of machine

walk and crawl unconsidered
the hard carapace, this city

where the vendors say the Bible
and American flag are always hot items.

Even if the world is finished,
snow falls on Columbus, Ohio.

Behind plastic, light-in-light-
blooming arc welders

promise superabundance
for a handful whose lives

rise piece by beautiful piece
at the decibel level of traffic.

Reinvention the rule, who
takes dominion does so by inches,

air and water
and imprecise earth overthrown,

patinaed bench attesting
quietly

to the persistence of what we put here.
What is not acceded to

becomes another's freezing vision:
wide-bodied ascensions into skyline,

closing margin between field
and field. Indigenous spin a cocoon

against the spew and plenitude.
Call it adaptation. Wings of snow

on I-beams
blacken and are replaced all day.

The Gift of Fury

What drove him on was the most ancient
cry of all, the cry to live, to take
the one life and give it all he had.
                    —Melvyn Bragg. *Richard Burton: a Life*

She is Sex and whispers hotly
in a voice as old as copulation that she is.
E.—his affectionate abbreviation
hinting at Eve, Eternal, Excess.
After the bathing scene in *Cleopatra*
—the hair, eyes, hint of breast—
he was lost. The troublesome Body
prevailed: Bloody Marys at ten thirty,
cracking the seal on a second fifth of vodka
by mid-afternoon. Tonight, boozing,
in the company of strangers,
he hears again a poet and friend:
Your pain shall be a music in your string
And fill the mouths of heaven with your tongue.
Like a boy shouting from a seat in a theater:
"Bloody love!" The light of the production
bathing him in unreality, erotic fundamentalism.
And the face: pock-marked, scarred,
lined by laughter and drink and story,
wreathed in smoke and the talk of men
conspiratorially confirming their worst fears
about her, about him. The Voice has him
and erupts in "How to Handle a Woman".
He sings as he lives, the song bursting
with this Welsh miner's son. And E.
Holding court on a sofa, jet-haired,
jewelled, the Sleeping Princess
waiting the rough kiss of the naked-in-spirit.
O but the room envies his immersion, hers,
the undiscovered countries of them.

The song ended, he recites *Ulysses*.
Whatever name you give it, this is acting:
braving those hard-edged jungles of language,
the old wars of words leading to an image
of one bending to love, lowering herself
onto that conventional wisdom we call sex.
E., wise in the body, full of the mystery
of any two of us, recipient of the catholic lusts
of America, the world, is entirely his.
Her legs lift in that infinite variety
of the animal. The left drifts from the right,
opening that accident of shadow and freed light
above stockings. Any future will do.

On a September Morning above a Pasture near Dayton, Ohio, Orville Wright Accomplishes His First Figure Eight

What we want is the romance.
Something on the order of Otto Lilienthal's
twelve-second soaring above the hills
outside Berlin, paying with his life.
Something of the fevered ache
and invisible fist flings you up
to the Nothing you'd faced before intuition
or invention, before you'd traced this
symbol of the Infinite above the early risers.
Admit that by some magic a bicycle builder
circles Huffman's Prairie, turns
above the thorny honey locust.
Spare us the mathematics and glamorless
theoretical discussions in the parlor
of the house on Hawthorn Street.
The prop noise and fuel stink
of days it wasn't glory so much as overcoming.
Tell us the name of the woman. Not
the durability of spruce versus pine spars,
that the total wing area of the 1903 Flyer
was more than five hundred square feet,
that "respectable members of the middle class
wore suits and hats in all weather in those days."
Surely somewhere by the fence, neck craning
heavenward, the shy lover of one or the other
reticent Wright waits with perfect patience.
We want to believe in motives we can identify
and own as heroic, human. A lust for fame
won't wash. Not with Wilbur outwitting
reporters, shooing them like Huffman's cows
with incessant tinkering when what they want,
what we want, are memorable lines about release,
the feel and poetry of flying, for Chrissakes.
Whatever our wishes, it's his show.

His neighborhood and bag of tricks,
his white Pride of the West muslin,
his airborne glimpse of the Dayton,
Springfield and Urbana Interurban Railway,
his lazy ferry of sunlight and sound,
his luck and cartoonishly average looks,
his usual, shaky climb up the sky,
his restrained smile all the way down.

The Boss Says He May Not Let the Cowboys In Next Year

Send a message to my heart...
—Dwight Yoakam

She describes infinity with a country song.
The song sounds like looking down
and seeing her beneath you, heaving breasts
and happy for this intermission
in the sorrowful arc of a life. She's
bending the clear night of the notes,
she's patient with the rowdy razzle-dazzle
of balding lawyers who could care less
that Patsy Cline rerecorded this one
thirty times to get it just so.

Blue is what we are, literally,
islanded in the trapped smoke and loungelight.
White is what she is—white lizard boots
white sequined mid-calf length cowgirl skirt
with white fringe. Mister, you can see
desire release in thinly guarded moments
in a supper club in Childress, Texas.
Of course you want her. For as long
as the evening lasts and the next song
of desolation fits perfectly an idea

of loneliness that is one to live through,
not this other that defeats you, all of us,
and is why we're here at this west Texas night's
Inaugural Ball for the Truly Lonely.

She's doing her best Marilyn Monroe, vamping
that old black magic a woman like this
enframes the world with. If it's sticky-
sweet dreams you want, you've come to the right place.
Tonight the pre-fab Elvis-on-velvet architecture

reverberates with the worst organ accompaniment
since the First Baptist Church let go that fellow
who said *So when, Mrs. Dixon, was the last time*
you say God said everything was just peachy?

Tonight the boss says he may not
let the cowboys in next year, he says
they don't spend like the lawyers
and that they're harder on the place.
He's doused the parking lot's gravel
with the light of mercury vapor lamps.
He's been watching how much whiskey I pour,
says he's liable and I say, *for what?*

To the problem of the cowboys, I say
their forearms smoothed the wood of the bar,
their boots the dancefloor's every board.
They drank all they could hold for years.
Sure, they pissed in the sinks, on the walls,
carved the names of sweethearts and FUCK YOU
so deep in the old wood it will be there
long after this new singer is neither new
nor singing. The boss won't listen.

He's from Ohio and an ex-marine. He's
fucking the singer, I heard. Hates Texas.
You can't tell him anything.

BOTTOM DOG PRESS
Supporting the Art of Literature
in the Midwest